Wild Britain

Woodlands

Louise and Richard Spilsbury

H www.heinemann.co.uk
Visit our website to find out more information about Heinemann Library books.

To order:
☎ Phone 44 (0) 1865 888066
📄 Send a fax to 44 (0) 1865 314091
💻 Visit the Heinemann Bookshop at www.heinemann.co.uk to browse our catalogue and order online.

First published in Great Britain by Heinemann Library,
Halley Court, Jordan Hill, Oxford OX2 8EJ
a division of Reed Educational and Professional Publishing Ltd.
Heinemann is a registered trademark of Reed Educational & Professional Publishing Ltd.

OXFORD MELBOURNE AUCKLAND JOHANNESBURG BLANTYRE
GABORONE IBADAN PORTSMOUTH (NH) USA CHICAGO

Designed by Celia Floyd
Illustrations by Alan Fraser
Originated by Dot Gradations
Printed in Hong Kong/China

ISBN 0 431 03904 6
05 04 03 02 01
10 9 8 7 6 5 4 3 2 1

British Library Cataloguing in Publication Data
Spilsbury, Louise
    Woodlands. – (Wild Britain)
    1. Forests and forestry – Great Britain – Juvenile literature
    2. Forest ecology – Great Britain – Juvenile literature
    I. Title II. Spilsbury, Richard
    577.3'0941

Acknowledgements

To our own young wildlife enthusiasts, Miles and Harriet.

The Publishers would like to thank the following for permission to reproduce photographs:
Bruce Coleman: Stephen Bond p9, Konrad Wothe p20, John Cancalosi p26, Hans Reinhard p28; Corbis/FLPA: B Borrel Casals p17, Hal Horwitz p19; Garden & Wildlife Matters: p13, p23, p29; NHPA: David Woodfall p4, Stephen Dalton pp11, 22; Oxford Scientific Films: Press-tige Pictures p5, Mark Hamblin p6, Tim Shepherd pp7, 27, Niall Benvie p8, Colin Milkins p10, G I Bernard p12, Ronald Toms pp14, 15, London Scientific Films p16, K G Vock p18, Terry Heathcote p21, Irvine Cushing p24, Tom Ulrich p25

Cover photograph reproduced with permission of Images

Our thanks to Andrew Solway for his comments in the preparation of this book.

Every effort has been made to contact copyright holders of any material reproduced in this book. Any omissions will be rectified in subsequent printings if notice is given to the Publisher.

Contents

Any words appearing in the text in bold, **like this,** are explained in the Glossary.

What is a woodland?

There are areas of woodland all over Britain.

Woodlands are areas of land covered with trees. Trees are tall plants with thick **trunks**, long branches and leaves.

A habitat provides living things with food, water and **shelter**. This badger lives in a woodland habitat.

A **habitat** is the natural home of a group of plants and animals. In this book we will look at a few of the plants and animals that live, grow and **reproduce** in a woodland habitat.

Types of trees

The leaves on deciduous trees are broad and flat.
Deciduous trees are sometimes called 'broad-leaved'.

There are two kinds of trees in woodlands
in Britain. **Deciduous** trees, like beech, oak
and ash, lose all their leaves in autumn.

The leaves on this Scots pine tree are dark green. They are long and thin like needles.

Coniferous trees, like pine, spruce or fir, do not lose all their leaves at the same time. The leaves are green all year round.

Changes

The deciduous trees in this wood have hardly any leaves by winter.

In autumn the leaves on **deciduous** trees change colour and fall. The fallen leaves make a damp, shady **habitat** for many minibeasts to live in.

When bluebells and other flowers die, their **roots** stay in the soil, ready to grow again next spring.

In spring, before new leaves grow big enough to block the light, sunlight reaches the woodland floor. Flowers thrive because they need this sunlight to grow.

Living there

Animals whose food grows on trees, are themselves food for larger birds and mammals.

Woodlands provide food and **shelter** for many animals. In the trees, leaves, flowers, **fruits**, **seeds** and nuts are food for **insects**, birds and **mammals**.

Minibeasts help to rot woodland waste. They **recycle** some of the goodness back into the soil.

Animals such as deer, foxes and badgers live at ground level. Worms, centipedes, ants and beetles live in the damp soil and rotting leaves on the woodland floor.

Trees

Where the seeds land, new coniferous trees may grow.

All trees **reproduce** by spreading **seeds**. The seeds of **coniferous** trees are in their cones. The seeds are blown out of the cones by the wind.

When ripe, beech fruits open to release the seeds.

The seeds from **deciduous** trees are in their **fruits**. In beech trees the fruit has a spiky outer case. This protects the seeds inside.

Fungi and ferns

Fungi, like these fly agaric, have a network of **root**-like threads hidden in the soil or among rotting leaves.

Fungi are plant-like living things. Mushrooms and toadstools are fungi. Fungi get the **nutrients** they need by feeding on dead leaves and dead animals on the woodland floor.

Ferns uncurl as they grow towards what light there is on the woodland floor.

Trees block light from the woodland floor, so few plants grow there. However, ferns and mosses thrive in these dark and damp conditions.

Woodlice and centipedes

Woodlice have hard shells to protect them against spiders that try to eat them.

Many minibeasts, like woodlice, find **shelter** under stones or bits of fallen **bark**, or in rotting leaves. Woodlice feed on rotting wood and other plants.

A centipede **poisons** and kills with its front pincers.

This centipede has 30 legs and moves quickly. It squeezes its flat, thin body under stones, bark and leaves and through soil. It eats **insects**, worms, spiders and slugs.

Ants and sawflies

Wood ants collect fallen leaves and rotten wood to make their nests.

Wood ants live in large groups in big nests on the woodland floor. They work together to kill caterpillars and moths. By killing these leaf eaters, ants protect the trees.

The young that **hatch** out of the eggs eat the needles.

Pine sawfly live and **reproduce** in pine woods. Females cut open pine needles and lay their eggs inside. The female's egg-laying tube has a jagged edge like a saw.

Warblers and goldcrests

The male wood warbler sings to attract a female.

Many birds, including wrens, chaffinches and great tits, live in woodlands. Most woodland birds **reproduce** in spring. Wood warblers build nests in beech trees so the leaves safely hide them from their enemies.

This goldcrest is feeding insects to its chicks.

The male goldcrest has brightly coloured head feathers to attract a female. Goldcrests build nests in old rotting pine trees to hold their eggs.

Owls and woodpeckers

Owls have huge eyes to help them see tiny animals in the dark.

Woodland birds find food in different ways. Tawny owls feed at night. They fly silently through the wood, listening out for tiny **mammals** below.

22

In woodlands you can sometimes hear the loud tapping as a woodpecker pecks holes in a tree.

A great spotted woodpecker breaks holes in tree **bark** using its sharp beak. It reaches into the cracks to pick out minibeasts like centipedes and woodlice to eat.

Badgers and pine martens

Badgers come out from their setts at night to eat nuts, beetles, slugs and worms, and to drink from puddles.

Badgers live under the woodland floor in setts. A sett is a maze of tunnels and rooms that badgers dig between the **roots** of trees. Badgers spend their days below ground.

Holes in trees provide safe, dry places to live.

Pine martens search the branches of trees for eggs, birds and other **mammals** to eat. They live and give birth to their young in holes in **coniferous** trees.

Deer and dormice

The spots on a fallow deer's back look like light shining down through the trees.

Fallow deer are large **mammals** that live in groups in woodlands. They eat grasses and ferns. They hide from danger among the trees and bushes.

The dormouse sleeps through the winter in a nest made out of leaves and tree **bark**.

A dormouse is a small, tubby mammal. Dormice are good climbers. They search the trees for nuts and **seeds** to eat.

Dangers

Trees take many years to grow, but can be cut down in a few minutes.

Many woodlands have been cut down to clear land for farms, factories and houses. When trees are destroyed, the plants and animals that live there lose their homes and their food supply.

These trees have been damaged by rain that was poisoned by pollution.

Factories, cars and power stations pump out smoke and fumes that cause air **pollution**. This makes rain so **poisonous** it can damage or even kill trees.

Food chains

All plants and animals in a woodland **habitat** are linked through the food they eat. Food chains show how different living things are linked. Here is one example.

Woodpeckers eat centipedes.

Centipedes eat woodlice.

Woodlice feed on rotting leaves and wood.

The artwork on this page is not to scale.

Glossary

bark the tough outer layer that covers a tree's trunk, branches and twigs

coniferous trees that don't lose all their leaves at the same time. They usually have leaves like needles.

deciduous trees that lose all their leaves in autumn. They usually have wide, flat leaves.

fruit the part of a plant or tree that holds its seeds

habitat the natural home of a group of plants and animals

hatch to be born from an egg

mammals group of animals that includes humans. All mammals feed their babies on milk and have some fur or hair on their bodies.

nutrients food that gives living things the goodness they need to live and grow

poison/poisonous chemical that can damage or kill living things

pollution something that poisons or damages air, water or land

recycle change waste into something that can be used again

reproduce when plants and animals make young just like themselves

roots parts of a plant that grow underground. They take in water and nutrients from the soil.

seeds these are made by a plant and released to grow into new plants

shelter somewhere safe to stay, live and have young

trunk main stem of a tree

Index